MUSEUM

MUSEUM

Frances Samuel

 TE HERENGA WAKA
UNIVERSITY PRESS

Te Herenga Waka University Press
Victoria University of Wellington
PO Box 600, Wellington
New Zealand
teherengawakapress.co.nz

Te Herenga Waka University Press
was formerly Victoria University Press.

A catalogue record is available at the National Library of New Zealand.

ISBN 9781776920020

Printed in Singapore by Markono Print Media Pte Ltd

for Eddie

Contents

SUPER(NATURAL) WORLD

(IM)MATERIAL WORLD

OBJECT LESSONS

Exhibition (*Security*)

The 'Gallery Guidance' sign said to supervise your children
and I did, oh, I kept my hands close to my sides.
But those red herrings of history –
well I whistled and through the alarm rays they swam.
I was above suspicion, just a trail of red pen
and some loose-limbed tears,
my employee's tag a cheap necklace
with an outdated cameo.
Outside in the wind, artefacts whirl in my coat pockets.
A spine from an extinct hedgehog, a fossilised bowtie,
an inch of elixir in a blue glass bottle.
If you ask me about the low pay
then I say I do it for love.
Let me show you,
just put your lips together like this –

SUPER(NATURAL) WORLD

Grateful to the Cactus

Sitting between a camel's humps
on the first day rain has ever rained
in this desert. The need for an oasis extinguished.
The clouds like grapes, darkening
just by looking at each other.

It seems that everything is clearer
without the rising heat waves.
Instead, a loud hissing sound
as every cactus lets go of its breath.

For the first day in forever
they don't have to be life savers,
sentinels of water, amenable
to the punctures of thirsty travellers.
Today the sky and its army of raindrops
can take care of everyone.

Your camel makes its slow way past
the tallest cactus in sight,
whose green arms, usually upright in surrender,
have deflated by its sides.

From your double mountaintop, you reach out
and shake its hand between spikes, saying
good job, thank you for your efforts!
In the world where you come from
you're told that everyone, apparently everyone,
likes to hear those words.

Water Bear

The water bear is a flattened cloud
on a glass slide rule.
It's hard to make out legs or even a head.
The water bear needs to moult in order to grow,
which reminds me of James saying
'It's the letting go that counts.'
If you are less than a millimetre long
is it possible to have days where you don't know
what to do with yourself?

Time to get some sunshine, and it's not far
from the science collections to the staff kitchen.
Someone – who? – has made soup,
turning over and over in the pot.
Soup is indestructible and water bears
can survive the vacuum of space.
They live on the film of water
around moss and lichen
and drying up for decades doesn't kill them.
Add water and off they go again.

Sometimes the lighter the more lasting.
I hold the slide rule to the window
and loosen my grip, but I'd never let the glass drop.
No need to write another exhibition label.
I could just lick the water bear
and set it free.

Tramping

Yesterday you were moss,
absorbing everything.
Today you don't want to learn
anything new.
You have your tin cup filled with ice
that doesn't feel like turning into water.
It's not personal.
The ice isn't trying to kill you.
In fact, a short walk away is a waterfall
and now it's a good thing
you're no longer moss
because moss doesn't have legs.
When you get there, thousands of drops
rain down on the thousands of people
gathered with their tin cups.
The sound is like clapping
and because you are empty
you make the most noise.

Exhibition (*Biomimicry*)

These herbarium specimens have led more exciting lives
than any of us, says Leon.
They travelled on Cook's voyages in the 1700s –
The light is shining on us as we listen
but not through us in the way
sunlight filters through leaves.
We can't have that until we're skeletons.

There is a word for the fading colour of a leaf as it dies.
I am thinking how maybe I am also captive to paper,
stuck on and identified, illustrated
and tied to a rope ladder of classification.
It's true the museum is a family tree
but it's often getting pruned.
Below, we are bruised and battered
by our fellow leaves, falling too early, still green,
and there aren't many of us.
I'm keeping the word count down
lower and lower as attention spans dissipate.
But it's not really about that.

It's about trying to read standing up
when you are tired from finding a car park,
or a child is pulling on your arm
and if you follow that child
you will see something magical
because children are divining rods,
always bending to the source.

Follow a child and they will lead you down
to look at a leaf next to an ant

being swept over by a shadow,
and you will miss the Terracotta Warriors
you will miss Monet and Mana Whenua
and the wedding dresses from the V&A
because we are all missing something
when we choose to follow a child.

Look at me: I put down my pencil,
I put down all the tools of all the trades.
I turned, and what is this new
kind of stone I've become?
that builds itself upwards
and warms with the sun
and moves.

Whairepo

In the lagoon outside the museum
a whairepo flaps
more like ululates.
It moves like a singing voice
if you could see a voice
and it could breathe underwater.

Someone is directing the whairepo
remote control.
Its skeleton is made of LED cables
tethered to the bottom of the lagoon.
You could say anchored
but that implies something solid
with no blood on the end of the line.

I guess one of the body's purposes
is to stop a song from floating away completely.
The remote control sends its signal
and the whairepo glides upwards
almost close enough to touch.

Not everyone learns to open their eyes underwater.
But the ears are open.
If someone could make you turn around
by lighting up your bones
you might risk opening your mouth after all this time.
You might break the surface with a low, low note.

Exhibition (*Limits*)

People once understood that if your body is 72.8 percent water
then the waxing moon is going to pull your blood
through your veins like the tides,
and the saliva in your mouth will soften your tongue
making you say things that the next month you'll regret.
But by then those words are fishes with their own brief lives
'leaping on a prehistoric sea where a colossal penguin looks up
from chasing a sea lion to swallow them whole.'

Alan found some colossal penguin bones in a rock
fossilised with words inside their immense densities.
You might use dynamite, you might use acetic acid
and a diamond saw – getting fossils out is a big job
because those things you said weren't meant to be repeated,
not then, and not 60 million years later.

On the ancient map, ancient penguins have a limit
to how far north they'll go.
Also marked is the 'southernmost limit of all reptiles'
along with the 'mock sun' and 'permanent snow'.
The map says you have to step backwards
to find yourself amongst the stars.
Lots of them, one of you. Is that a good thing?
Getting things in perspective and feeling outnumbered
are two different things.

On the flip side, in the deep sea
becoming gigantic
comes down to a set of circumstances.
If you had more oxygen and space and the right temperature
you too could become a giant scale worm

that protects itself with iridescent scales that fall off
during battle, making a predator's grip slide.
The relief of escape makes you unrecognisable
for the few minutes before whatever is protecting you
and whatever is bothering you grows back.

Go lower on the map and the air itself is an archive
trapped in ice, the bubbles holding gases
and viruses, evidence of hurricanes.
If ice can tell us so much
without moving its lips,
then those bones releasing their words
might still cause an explosion.

Climate Change

Since we are all made up of atoms and vibrations,
let's rearrange ourselves.
You be a bird and I'll be a buffalo,
stand on my back and off we go, carefully
stepping over our discarded clothes.

We are six-legged and four-eyed
and if you flap your wings, little bird,
those raindrops will lift us up
on their return to the clouds
– then we'll really be away.

Someone else we know
has become an alpine goat.
We meet on a mountain
to talk about where to go next
and who to be when we get there.

From above, we watch travellers on the trails
tying and retying their loads to donkeys' backs.
They take a few steps and the load slips again.
Over and again, agreement can only come
when the bird in me bleats
to the buffalo in you.

The Safest Place

The lightning field is not a magical place.
Over the length of a day, the worms
often fail to raise their heads
from the shocked earth.

When a team of foragers comes from the city
in their hired minivan
they make note of the singed birdsong
then bend down to business.
Plant life survives here and its anxious, smoky leaves
are like gold on the restaurant market.

Somebody warned the foragers
a sign of lightning was clouds growing tall
in a windy, darkening sky.
Someone else said just run
so both your feet aren't on the ground
at the same time.

Neither of these things happen
when the flash comes.
But those worms that were playing dead
are suddenly sitting inside the minivan
with all the windows rolled up.

Fast Forest

The words are falling from him like seeds.
They are growing from the ground
in a fast forest. He talks so much
new species are sprouting to keep up.
Maybe this verbose forest has medicines
in its leaves and berries, or saps
that are poisonous.
There are reasons why a forest stops growing
in the line where it does.
Outside this border there are hostile lands.
If he wants to go any further
he will need to be brave;
he will need to start singing.

Seed/Leaf/Tree

All this death hardly matters
when you are in the forest.
For every tree you see
there are at least a hundred more,
waiting in the soil.

A seed is just as alive
as the tree that towers over it.
It is waiting for the trigger to grow.
A kōwhai seed can wait a hundred years,
no problem.

*

The weight of a leaf is what makes it bend
and snap from the branch.
Rake some leaves into a pile and you'll see
each one shows a clean break
in the same place near the base of the stem.

If one hundred thousand leaves
can make a clean break every day
then what are you waiting for?

*

It's rare, but a tree can be in two places at once.
What was once a twig
can be forced to function as a trunk.
Much like you who have gone
floating off down the river

scrambled up the bank and planted yourself –
twig into trunk.

Now that you have new resources
your choices are the same
as any other:
grow, repair, defend, reproduce.

Only I know you will choose the fifth action,
which is to delay indefinitely,
storing your earnings
for later mobilisation.

In this same way, I will go the short distance
from standing under a tree
to being the tree,
trusting the light to tell me
when winter is coming.
Not the weather.

And despite the fact that most seeds get no trigger,
already I am throwing down hundreds more.
The seeds underneath me
are in pain in the earth.
They have so much to do:
cells dividing, seeking light, splitting open.

Tornado

I don't know when the tornado is coming
so I open all the windows and doors.

I've heard by doing this the introverted wind
will funnel through the house

and out the other side
rather than lifting it off its foundations.

Well that turned out to be
an old man's tale.

I sit here on the last stool
a chicken in my hands somehow

its feathers spiralling off
like a plague of unknown insects.

This shivering bird
is the only thing left for miles

with warm blood that moves.
Still –

if that tornado had left me a pot
this chicken would be in it.

Exhibition (*Bees*)

Here's a lost tour group in the staff lift
on the way to Level 3 with me.
Back of house seemed more interesting than front of house.
But I had to tell them, didn't I? the right way to go.
I had to send them out into *Blood Earth Fire*.

Below on Level 2, Te Taiao Nature,
the Haast's eagle with its three-metre wingspan
is carrying another visitor away to a mountaintop.
The moa's extinction will eventually take with it
the hungry Haast's, its faithful predator,
along with the parasite species that lived on its body.
The person on the mountaintop is calling,
the sound like those parasites running,
spreading from the last moa body
like a pool of black blood with nowhere to go.

A change in direction to Level 6
and a view to the ocean.
Somewhere out there a humpback whale mother
is whispering to her newborn a warning about sharks.
Who would believe that a whale could whisper,
but it can. In the same way, I will save your life
a thousand times, my breath gentle
on the seashell of your ear.
Somehow – how? – I'll make it so safe
even the waters surrounding you will fall asleep.

Level 5, Toi Art, and the air conditioning's cold enough
to overcome curiosity. I'm talking in a quiet voice,
the one I use when there's a lot to say

but I can't say everything.
Step back into the lift, heading downwards,
there's yellow-black caution tape
to stop people closing their hands in the doors.

Level 1, cafe, shop, and automatic exit–entrance.
Two native bees hover by the glass doors
humming not whispering, their tongues
too short for the introduced flowers.
The difference between me and a visitor
is that a visitor walks slowly.
Today I'm walking slowly enough
to look one of those hungry bees in the eye.
I see my reflection in the glass, almost cross-eyed.
I look like a person with the shadow
of an eagle overhead. I look like a person
who's trying to hear a whale whisper.
I look like a person who needs someone
to show them the way out.

Essential Tremor

Your hand shakes when you try to hold it still.
They say that's how your drawings talk about
both physical and existential pain.
In the meantime, I'm writing
about volcanoes, earthquakes, tsunami.

The mechanical wave in the tank
hits the shore and some people
standing with a horse (in the city!)
get washed over and over.
The longer you look through the glass
the more it feels like it is you getting wet.

It doesn't help that taniwha are carrying their fire
through the underworld to warm you.
Even if the fire found a way to ride the horse
or the horse found a way to ride the fire
that wave would keep coming.

So it's better you are now inside the glass
rather than outside looking in.
Because inside the glass box of the museum
the idea is that everything we love survives.

(IM)MATERIAL WORLD

Robotics

The robotics scientist thinks we could learn more
from the body. The way it forgets after a moment
the feeling of clothes pressing against it.
He left school aged nine, planted trees and built log cabins,
disappointing his parents by not becoming an artist.
Now his research is paid for by the military
and he says it's a good thing we're so far behind
and can't yet make robots
that are killing machines.

It's true there are times to feel
and times not to feel
in this season of unusual brightness.
While the sun is out, we lift up
anything uncovered about ourselves
– faces, throats, regrets –
to feel the heat of those rays completely.

The robotics scientist says we can't tickle ourselves
because you can't surprise your own body.
The body always knows what's coming.
When, body?
When will the robots come?

Radiant Hospitality

I'm in my house listening to the owls calling.
The moon shines on the ghosts
reclining on the couch, on the La-Z-Boy chair.
They have outstayed their welcome.

To get rid of these ghosts
I have to lift off the roof
turn the house over
and shake them out like salt.

Soon after, the living come knocking.
And I, with my radiant hospitality, say
'Come in, sit down. Tea or coffee?'
The living: they wonder, but they never ask,
why the seats are warm.

How to Catch and Manufacture Ghosts

I offer a right of return. Thirty days, or more like forty, taking into account wanderings in the desert. Bed sheets with elasticated corners are the best tools for the job. Throw one in the air, watch it billow like a jellyfish, then wait for the snag. If it moulds slightly in the shape of a figure, you've got one. Gotcha. You don't say that out loud.

White sheets never did so well in the desert. I didn't do so well either. There were shimmerings in the distance but they were all bottle tops. Tops without the bottles. When I came out of the desert I was sunburnt and tired and I decided enough is enough: I'm going to start my own business, be my own boss, which is where the ghost-catching came in. Never had to advertise. Lots of ghosts around, just confusing people's lives.

Where's your net, my customers say when I come to the front door. They want to see me carrying a big gossamer butterfly-catching net over my shoulder like Huckleberry Finn. But they stop worrying when my sheet starts floating down, hypnotically slow and quiet.

Most ghosts don't struggle. I think they're happy to be caught. I've only once tried to let one go. The customer said: It's my wife – well, if she wants to stay she can stay. But that ghost, by the shape of it, she did the fingers under the sheet at her husband. He laughed, the sheet shook too, and I thought this job is anything but predictable, it's not your nine to five, although I do keep those hours. Then the husband he was sob-laughing and the sheet was maybe sniffling and I don't do this often but I left my toolkit there and went outside.

I opened the back of my van – the model is actually called a 'Fun Cargo' – then when the couple were both ready they came out and got in. And now it's a real dilemma for me which way to drive because, as you know, the dead are going one way and the living are going another.

Mr Bones

What's it like to be always night?
The bats hanging from the trees outside the museum
speaking a language so plain
dogs and cats can understand it.

There's a man hanging with the bats
in the trees, upside down, not dead.
He has suffered an irreversible loss
and talks about himself
sometimes in the third person
sometimes in the second.

He has a friend, never named,
who addresses him as Mr Bones
and feeds him small pieces of bread
he will not choke on
like his father did that wishbone.

Mr Bones could touch down
in a shaky handstand, and topple
back into the upright world, easily.
The bats are used to him
but they wouldn't miss him.

Try as he might he can't perfect sleeping,
wrapped up in himself
and every dream a cacophony
of blood to the head.

He's not hopeless,
he just can't think straight.

And as long as he stays hanging in the trees,
only a few sniffing dogs to bother him –
on good days, the moon and the sun
just a glimpse between leaves –
he doesn't have to.

Life-drawing Class

The book said if you wanted a cow
you drew the cow.
And if you wanted the milk
you drew the milk.
And if you didn't want that snowflake anymore
you simply joined the points together
to make a spider's web.

On the course, the advanced students would draw the sun
then smudge the edge of the circle
to warm up the room.
The same technique made a star shoot,
then you could wish on it – for anything.
I sensed the power of what I was learning.

There was one rule: you couldn't erase.
If you didn't like something you drew,
if the elbows of that tree were stabbing birds,
you had to keep drawing.
'Draw again. Draw better' was the tagline.

But if an online class has a back corner, then I was in it.
I was flailing in a whirlpool of my own sketching.
I had to draw my mum to get me out.

As she spoke, full of concern,
I drew some coins: soothing, repetitious rounds.
Mum recited my student debt (my age plus three zeros),
and lack of pitched roof, weatherproof shoes, pot-luck dinner invites.
Boy, those coins were really mounting up!

I ran their coolness through my fingers.
Mum tested the metal with her teeth.

Every pencil in my pocket – HB, 2B –
I threw them away like crutches,
and I filled my pockets with my new wealth.
Then I drew the river and walked into it.

Overcoming Regret

Wherever he goes, an elephant tags along.
In another story, it is a pile of wood.
Logs roll off and crush
his trailing shadow into dust
left for the street-sweeper van
that rumbles along the gutters at 1am
waking the tourists in their hotel beds.

Meanwhile the elephant
has chewed the leaves from every tree it passes.
Its leader does not notice.
But now that the trees are naked behind him
and the elephant is full
the rest is easy.

Tree with Bird

> What bird would light
> in a moving tree
> the tree I carry
> for privacy?
>   —Lorine Niedecker

I guess that bird
thought I might be going
someplace interesting.

This tree is not a journey –
it is hiding me! I say to the bird,
quick to point out that rhyme
is not something I strive for.

We wait together, by the letterbox.
The tree, which stands tall
as if planted in the sky by its leaves,
has barely enough trunk to hide my eyebrows.

There's nothing to do then, bird,
except keep close to home.
I myself spend quite some time here
in the backyard, by the coop,
sewing clothes for the chickens.
But not a damn one of them
will put their trousers on.

Paper-cut Skeleton

Tiny nicks in the fingers, held breath –
all to make a skeleton stand up

her heels still attached to the page
her bones like cobwebs

that would tear
if the spider sneezed

her heart a negative space
behind ribs, vibrating in the dark air.

If this skeleton walked off the page
and turned up at a Day of the Dead party

just the suggestion of grief
would make her sink to her knees

her bones damp, too heavy
to rise again.

Painting

The painter painted a half rhino, half zebra.
Nobody bought it
since it was neither one thing nor the other.

A poet saw the painting resting on the easel
and recognised an animal
that could both dazzle and charge.

With an archaic whistle, she called it
and it came to her.
On the animal-shaped emptiness left on the canvas

she wrote a poem – her best yet.
But nobody bought the poem-painting either,
since it was neither one thing nor the other.

Moonhoppers

Windy night and the orange and green
moonhoppers roll around the deck.
Rain is hole-punching its way in.
It might get here before the stars –
the struggle for visibility goes beyond
a human concern.
I'm too tall now to ride a moonhopper.
A trip to space is no longer a possibility.
Still, I'm hoping to see the stars for a second
before the rain starts to tell its life story
on my upturned face.
I've thought about bringing the moonhoppers inside.
But in times like these, with so many of us
losing traction, there's a chance
someone might need a getaway vehicle.
Out here in the suburbs?
Okay, at the very least they might need
a pause, pause, pause
from life on Earth.
The orange moonhopper bounces the highest.
You knew without me telling you
that it would be the orange
and not the green.

Exhibition (*Colour*)

I can break you apart
by putting a prism in front of you.
Then from your pocket
you get out another prism
and put yourself back together.
Call it a parlour trick. Call it
there are things we need to talk about.

Forget gamma, X-ray, ultraviolet.
Infrared is a trap and radio waves
tell me nothing. Both of us
have a limited palette of impure pigments.
This is a problem.

The more colours we blend, the more likely
the end result will be murky.
Mixtures absorb more light wavelengths,
sucking the luminosity.
Is that how you think of me – a lux vampire?
History wanted brighter colours
and so do I, so do I.

To get these colours
we have to grind down rocks to powder
and handle poisonous raw ingredients,
visit alchemists, apothecaries,
and unscrupulous dealers called colourmen.

Yes my materials are shaping my art.
Readymade couldn't come fast enough,
nor could collapsible metal paint tubes.

Now I can work outside
with the most vibrant pigments ever seen.

In the Middle Ages, blue
was considered the hottest of colours.
This could mean everything is okay between us.
In the Quran, Bible, Icelandic sagas, Vedic chants,
there is no mention of the sky being blue.
If you don't have a word for something
it doesn't mean you can't distinguish it.

Yellow is yellow because it isn't red, blue, orange.
Different wavelengths are deflected
until it's only yellow that hits the brain.
Putting aside for the moment

that all colour is ambiguous, and most of the time
we're looking at the same colour
and seeing very different things,
yellow about sums you up:
the brightest and the last.

Miniature Sketch

Do the sketch
then make the real thing.

Did you do it?
Did you make the real thing?

Fashion

My friend wears a grass jumpsuit
teeming with ants and worms.
No one sits next to her on the bus
and that's how she likes it.

A passenger in cobwebs
thinks he's too good for her
until his spider defects to her greenery
and his threads fall into holes.

I sit at the back in my flowers.
It takes six wheelbarrows full
to cover a body my size.

At the front, the woman in the sack
is warm and sturdy.
The rain clouds are heavy,
heavy for days, and darkening.

When the bugs start running
from my friend's suit
each of us realises the error of our ways:
the delicate flowers, the fine grass,
the shimmering cobwebs.

The woman in the sack will outlast us all,
and when the puddles come
it will be the first time
she's looked in a mirror.

Exhibition (*Shoes*)

There is a realm of ice
and a realm of fire
and you have one foot in each.

One shoe is blue, the other red
and you move fast
because you want to warm up one foot
and put the flames out on the other.

In your haste, sparks fly
from the red shoe onto the blue shoe
and ice shards flick
from the blue shoe onto the red shoe.

There is smoke and steam
and without their fire and ice
the shoes are nothing at all.
You are barefoot with a long way to go.

The pathway turns from rocks to sand
to grass to gravel.
Then there is no path at all.

But there are trees
and you have wings, don't forget.
You can find your way in the night
by throwing your voice
and listening for how long it takes
to hit something.

In this forest, as in all forests,
there are more leaves than trunks.
Your voice passes through them
in a kind of music. Now comes
the bounce back –

Hustle your wings into action
and watch your head
because voices can't be trusted
and neither can solid matter
in these quantum times.

The next day those trunks might be wind
and for all your prenavigation
you might fly into a mountain.

From high up, the realms of ice and fire
don't look so separate anymore.
Warm wind rises from one end
and cold descends from the other
colliding to make a sort of canopy.

And suddenly it's a good thing
you extinguished your shoes
because now you are walking on air.
And when you are walking on air
you can go anywhere.

Pilgrims

He wants to keep his hands free
so he combs his memories into his hair
and sets off on the coastal route.
That's the last we'll see of him for months.

But here she comes, returning from the desert
dressed only in the sand the wind blew
against her body.

The sea is such a surprise to her.
She steps from wave to wave
before her feet remember
what it is to sink.

The sand washes away and she floats
with the sudden lightness of a loss
that has been coming for a long time.

Now he is back from his journey
along the edge of five oceans.
He has given up his freedom
for a fistful of sand

and he holds it out to her, saying
Did you drop this? Surely
this is yours.

Respite

A few days of sanity.
Then the dice rolls
on its own again.

Exhibition (*Parade*)

Today when a single raindrop
could knock you out of line,
you are walking in a parade
dressed as someone from forest folklore,
wearing a wreath and holding a candle.

In the antenatal class, the teacher said line up
in preference of home birth or hospital birth.
The two of you way down one end, out in the cold,
and that's where you stayed for the rest of the course.

The candles are lit but the dark holds back a little.
They say you should always do that
when you're telling the truth.

The parade is coming up to a roundabout
and the line needs to curve.
Too many feet trying to change direction.
As always you fall over, but this time
your light continues to carry itself

the way the parade was heading –
confident, in the way that only light is,
that you will get to your feet
and run to catch up.

It sounds it, but these things are never simple.
You will have to run all the way
without moving your arms or head,
so when you finally reach the light
you don't blow yourself out.

Breathing

My baby sleeps in another room
while I write. So many times,
I walk into the room
to check he is breathing.
So many times, I write four words
then check again that
when I read over my writing
it has the rhythm of breathing.
Eventually, when I leave the room
the words keep breathing on their own.
And so I stand between these two lives, listening.
Then suddenly I am running
running without rest
checking that neither stops.

Girls Standing on Lawns – Photographs

There's no use standing around
back to the trees, all dressed up
with your teeth on fire.

A ribbon, a uniform,
some colourised flowers to the left,
hands buried in topiary.
You are not in a costume.

Three girls, now two.
There will come a time
when you can't believe it's you
standing on that lawn.

Holding a flag, waist-length plaits
and a red tie. Someone asked us to do this.
We want to, or we would not
be standing here.

It doesn't have to be a lawn.
Stand on the nearest length of sky,
but stand for something!
Otherwise, why are you even standing?

This is the whole thing:
we believe nothing more at this moment.
All of us gone from here
and yet we are still standing.

Pottery

A pot explodes in the kiln
taking everything else with it.
Failure with clay is more complete
and more spectacular
than with other forms of art –
the best you can say about a failed poem
is that it 'sags'.
At low tide, you can find pottery fragments
but you can't take them
from this marine reserve.
You can walk off with a washed-up inner sole
in your size, or a barnacled dive compass.
Same with poetry fragments.
Those are yours to take
if abandoned to the sea,
lost on a long journey, then returned
to the sand, indifferent to discovery.
Pots are approachable, democratic, familiar to everyone.
They don't require special knowledge to interpret
and neither do poems.
Did I say a pot? I meant a poet.
A poet explodes at a kitchen table
taking everything else with her.

OBJECT LESSONS

The Kindness of Giants

At this moment, a committee
is discussing what to do with you.
Minutes are being taken. It starts to rain
and you open your arms to give shelter.

Your feet are shod in cruise ships, and your eyes
look through spectacles made of frozen lakes.
Trapped fish obscure your vision.

The poor are supposed to be invisible
but you can be seen from space.
Stonehenge teeth and nationwide shoulders.

The committee has an announcement.
They shout it upwards, their words
reaching as far as your kneecaps.

But you already know their decision.
And just then, with your head in the mountains,
you hold your breath as the tiny skiers pass by.

A New Body

Believe it or not, your lungs are six weeks old –
and your taste buds just ten days!
   —*Daily Mail*

Really, what do I have in common
with my body?
   —Anna Swir

I was walking through my veins
on the scenic route
to get acquainted with my new lungs,
untainted stomach, pristine kidneys.

Not the addictive type, organic
yet mindfully anxious,
I was taking the opportunity
to admire my efforts.

But the terrain was shadowy
and there were echoes.
Here spleen spleen spleen –
I attempted to call my organs to me
like small faithful dogs.
Not one responded.

When I had shuffled my way to my heart
I took a pause in chamber no. 3.
'Herb,' I said, using the first name that came to mind
because I was weary of being surrounded by strangers,
'Why'd you have to go and change?'

I guess what I was really trying
          trying   trying
to say was: This year was going well for us
– my body and I –
we were finally getting somewhere.
And now all this red blood
where there used to be blue.

Recommended Exercise

If you really, really don't have time
to exercise, stand in the living room
and wave your arms around like a conductor.

I tried that, because I had young children
and was in the really can't do it category
along with leaving the house
and sleeping.

But it's really wonderful.
Helen Simpson, the short story writer, asked
Why do we always need to qualify any complaint
about parenting like that?
It is possible to be very happy
and very miserable at the same time.
It's just easier to apologise
than describe the impossible.

The poet Pessoa has his own advice:
Stop moving your arms around so much.
Count to 12, he says, not understanding
that in the world you live, where Mummy counting
is a last-ditch way to get some pyjama pants on,
counting to 5 is the absolute limit.

Exhibition (*Explain Yourself to a Plant*)

The plant wants to transform what you're telling it
into light and water, like it does
with all things. It's not about you.

So let the full stop fall from your fist
where you have been squeezing it,
a faint ache in your palm.
That full stop needs to rotate
so it can finish things up –
not least your own story.

Maybe you're crying,
but plants never mind that!
When you wipe your eyes the sky has gone
and a freak of nature towers over:
a sunflower with multicoloured petals
and a black stem.

It cranes its immense face
down towards your face.
Up close, it has no scent.
Up close, you see the best thing.
The best thing is that
this brilliant expression of the past
has no seeds.

Exhibition (DNA)

> – you could think *random* but you know
> the patterns are there –
> —Adrienne Rich

Here I am now, taking off the washing-up gloves
on the move, because no matter how separate
we believe our souls to be
we've still got an obligation to sort things out.

After all, I've taken hold of the ends of this double helix
and if you grasp the other ends
we can turn this bendy ladder,
untwisting some of what we've done
or what your father or grandfather did.

No one will thank us for this. In future
they won't know we've saved them from a life
of sweeping blossoms into piles
and not knowing what to do with them.

Back to me, and I no longer hesitate
to climb onto the first rung, or the second.
I'm passing this freedom backwards
to previous generations. My anxious aunty
and sister in the car with the engine on.

Up here in the thin green air,
I'm feeling the wind on my face
with the joy of a dog on a family car trip,
head out the window.

Back to you, and you've let go of the ladder altogether
and spiral into the future
with the lightness of an astronaut
who will one day cover the entire Earth
with her thumb. Forgiveness

has a way of unfurling,
just when the cage doors are closing
and the blossoms blow overhead,
having lost their scent and with it
all power of destruction.

Exhibition (*Navigation*)

There is more than one way to navigate
and one of those is to wait
for the islands to move towards you.

Other times it's asking: how far have I come from home,
rather than how far is x, y, z from me?
Men with telescopes have become famous
for the latter. But those men were starving
on a sea full of sustenance
lost under a sky full of stars
pointing the way.

You who are new to these waters
think I don't know.
But I do know where the new worlds are.
And their treasures. All the various hoards.
I've seen them.
And I've kept nothing for myself.
And I'm not telling.

Coin Rubbings

You're putting pieces of paper over things.
When did that start? Coins are too obvious –
you're looking for the contours of joy or hope,
so you take your non-toxic beeswax crayon
and rub away at a recent memory: that Friday
your jacket dropped off your bike carrier
during a downhill into the city.
It was trapped among the leaves in the gutter
when you went searching for it hours later.
But what appears now under your paper
is not the wind-rolled jacket but a word:
relief.

Yesterday, you had a calm blue rectangle
over a simpler object – a bicycle made of wire –
and the rubbing revealed an ambulance.
Now you're walking everywhere, arriving late,
your feet longing for the Ferris wheel of the pedals
and your fingers for the tinny bell
that miraculously made person after person jump
and step aside. Jump and step aside.

Tree roots used to be a favourite
but lately they're throwing up maps of ancient lands.
The crayon you hold is barely a stub
and there's no way you can look for a buried civilisation
when the details of the present elude you.
Popular wisdom says to stop seeking outside yourself,
that it's all inside. So maybe it's as easy
as placing the paper over your own face

and rubbing to see what impression
you're making on the world.

Your dog is lying here sleeping, soft and safe,
so you put some paper over him
and rub for reassurance. But no,
it's a phoenix, not rising
but bursting into flames.
You pack the paper and crayons away
under the bed, before bandaging your burned hand.

In the spring, tulips and daffodils burst effortlessly from the ground.
You press a thin circle of newsprint to the Queen's fine head
because it's no longer out of the question
to rub a common coin.
The rubbing shows tails
and although it's supposed to be heads,
and tails often means losing,
you say I'll take it. I'll take the tails.
Close enough.

Centenarian

The interviewers line up
when you are 100.
But your friends are never at home.

Whakairo

We are all carved in such a way
that when we stand outside
the rain runs off us.
Down our foreheads, along our shoulders,
arms, and fingers.
In the same way, we are positioned
just a little off the ground
so the damp doesn't soak up
into our spirits.
We are carved like this so we will live
to tell our stories.
Different tools change the shape of the story.
The grooves deeper with metal, wider with stone,
or intricately eaten away by a grub.
And always a circle of iridescent pāua shell
laid on the tongue to remind us
that it is the gods who speak
and we who must listen.

You Bury Me

There is a hierarchy of burial:
goldfish before bird
cat before dog
parent before child.

It is only fair that the one
who is most difficult to live without
should stay the longest.

It is not so strange then
this strange ritual
where I open your hand
fill your palm with dirt
then tenderly close your fingers around it.

The Passionfruit Vine

I am tired and the baby sleeps.
I have made food and done dishes and clothes washing
and picked up the toys.
Today some trucks came and made hay
in the paddock behind
and the paddock in front.
Effortlessly, the trucks drove and rolled up the grass
then dropped drum-shaped bales
and drove on.
Later, in the garden, the baby and I shook the passionfruit vine
and looked in the grass for the fruit that had fallen.
Perfect purple ovals.
This discovery is the closest I've come
to understanding the thrill of gardening.
Surprise offerings, maybe nothing
then six brand new at once.
After months of ripening,
it seemed those green passionfruit
would never darken and spring from the vine.
But now, even though I am very tired,
if I go out and stand in the garden, and wait,
something will drop in the darkness.

Fatigue Font

I want to write about fatigue.
I can do this in Inherit or Liberation Serif.
Both fonts are relevant to the subject.

Insomnia is not voluntary
but when you are up
up up with a child in the night,
any non-sleeping by someone childless
looks like free will.

We've tried the hard-nosed approach,
I assure my mother,
and the soft-squirrel reassurance.
In the mornings we mumble and frown
in our moss-coloured dressing gowns.

There are a small, such a small, number of parents
who'll admit to sleepless children.
A few said theirs started sleeping at age five.
For us, that is seven hundred and thirty more nights
of unfinished dreams, unfinished everythings,
cold feet on the dark wood floor.

Last week on the downhill from Mount Cook
the sun was shining I was on my bike
speeding beautifully I closed my eyes for a second
I was asleep.
I have also fallen asleep between the floors of a lift.

Even now I am growing sleepy as the poem lengthens like a shadow.
Australian poet Gwen Harwood had four children

and wrote letters too, but replying was hard:
'I am generally so tired after dinner that I just long to curl up
in Plato's cave and watch the flickering images.'
Email feels too long, and that conversation
you're trying to have with me –
too long too.

If I again consider those font choices,
I think the appropriate one to use for this poem is Inherit.
All that time I spent knitting a soul together,
crafting eyeballs, smoothing the ends of ribs.
Nine months is just a snap of the fingers compared to the night –

but enough about that. This is my writing day!
Time for big themes, flickering images.
Is there any way I can fool myself
that by sleeping now I am actually writing?
A cave could mean bears, hibernation.
Hit 'save'. Close eyes. Liberation.

Red Whistle, Orange Lifejacket

Well you say you don't need me
to walk with you anymore.
That's okay because I have things to do,
things I put off because I couldn't put off
you growing up.

I get home too early and the rhythm is out.
You turn your small back and wave,
and I longed for this expanse, I did –
it won't take me long to get used to it.
I'll be 20 again, doing two loads of washing in a row
and thinking I was busy.

I guess you can cross roads alone.
I used to be able to but now something is missing
without your little hand in mine.
I'm forever in Island Bay trying to get across the rivers:
Liffey, Mersey, Tiber, Clyde.

We can both fit in a dinghy, nothing fancy.
You're reaching out for the fluffy stalk of the toetoe
on council land. I'm supposed to be morally instructive,
I'm supposed to say you can't take it,
but I need a flag for this historic landing.

When we get there, I unclip my arms from around you.
I take my fluorescent, inflated self – provider of safety
and special cushioning at the back of the neck.
I take that stuff and leave you with the dangling red whistle
and no instructions, moral or otherwise,

because those whistles were so plastic, so weak
they barely made a sound.

Am I shouting this from water to land?
If I am it's because this is how it's always been
since you moored your first cell inside my body:
If you need me, you just breathe.

Black Book Blueprint

Books will be carbonised black bricks
thousands of years from now.
Something to stack up or burn,
their contents lost forever.

I've already got a blueprint
of the house I'm going to build
with all the books I wrote and didn't write –
in the future the realised and unrealised
are equally unreadable.

I'll run my fingernail along the black walls
and gather enough soot to keep writing.
From what used to be my books, I'll grind ash for tattoo ink.
Because in the future I have a new job,
and it's about skin not paper.

Back in paper times, I was looking for the vein
with my pencil on paper. I was pressing hard,
a pressure bump on my finger.
The words came up through the underside
and then I could relax. Then I could say,
there you are! like that famous sculptor
who took away from the stone everything
that was not the elephant.

But with tattooing, I'm realising
the more I take away from the body
the less tattoo there is.
I need to go back to writing.
Why is this always the way?

With the black books, I'm planning a staircase
for my new house. I'm up to 19 floors
and the view is getting thin. Like words on pages,
it doesn't go all the way to the edges.

This kind of house isn't going to increase in worth,
not even in a millennium.
I won't be able to pass it on to my children
because in the present I know
the most valuable objects
are the ones that remember their own stories.

Folding Tables

Please mind your fingers. To your right, the squat lobster in the display case. These all-seeing eyes gave spiritual protection to the warrior. Spectacular communities thrive around black smokers because they are like magical restaurants. Quirky egg-like figures choreographed by the wind. In particular, he is interested in what happens when the objects of memory no longer exist. Cut the text up and arrange it on the page with double-sided tape or rubber cement. Aztec priests would have understood the glyphs in this ancient codex but scholars today are still interpreting it. Unless otherwise stated, all prints in this touring exhibition were type-C prints made from digital scans of the original 35-millimetre negatives or transparencies. Rich rose pink is highlighted by a metal thread pattern symbolising moving water. The robes of Buddhist monks must be coloured using the dye from six particular plants. One ancestral figure stands above another. Around 1970, closed or full-face helmets were introduced, which defended the driver's head against flying objects, fire, and impact. In this world, all boundaries are lost. Grey and black lifeless palette of the rock face and the symbolism of the falling bird. The loss of something or perhaps someone important. Artists used ordinary household linoleum for the blocks, cutting the design with gouges made from the ribs of old umbrellas. If there is no wall stud or solid surface, a wall anchor can be used. Reverse side: An allegorical scene depicting a woman with a cornucopia. These lily ponds are details from the natural world, yet they also uncannily evoke the drift of planets through infinite space. The wedding guests, however, see something hidden from the viewer – they ignore their watermelon to watch Jesus intently. May our descendants live on and our hopes be fulfilled. If you had the chance, would you create a new identity? This group of gorilla-mask-wearing, anonymous feminist activists has been mocking the male-dominated art world since 1985. But not everything in the painting is as it seems. These skeletons were found fossilised in the muddy footprint of a massive sauropod dinosaur. Here, the even tension shows the steady hand of an experienced weaver. This was sci-fi for real. The Museum may share your contributions on social media. Sorry! Aroha mai. I am pakaru. Ko broken ahau. Sorry. The rest unknown. Thank you.

Museum Without an End

Inside me,
my heart
inside my heart
a museum
　　—Yehuda Amichai

Inside your heart, a museum
and not the free-entry kind,
not the kind with a rollercoaster
a cafe and a shop.
This museum has four rooms
and two are closed for renovations.
One is packed full of security guards
and the other has a black hole in the floor
the lighting technician refuses to spotlight.
It's hard to see any of the exhibits
because the walls shift and curve beyond view.
This museum asks too much of you.
There is a steep fee for coat check and no wayfinding.
By midday, the crowds have lost interest in trying
to reach the walls and stare instead
at each other's faces. This is okay
because inside the heart nothing is on display
that everyone hasn't seen before.
Now here comes one of those security guards
because – hey! – what are you doing
taking a run-up to that dark hole
and leaping like your life depends on it.

Notes and Acknowledgements

p.14: The line 'Add water and off they go again' and the information about water bears come from Phil Sirvid's blog post 'Fantastic Water Bears and How to Find Them': blog.tepapa.govt.nz/2017/08/15/fantastic-water-bears-and-how-to-photograph-them/

p.19: The phrases 'southernmost limit of all reptiles', 'mock sun', and 'permanent snow' are from *Animal Mineral Vegetable: Organising Nature: A Picture Album* (Wellcome Trust, 2016). The information about scale worms and ice comes from writing for Te Taio Nature, Museum of New Zealand Te Papa Tongarewa.

p.24: 'All this death hardly matters' and some other phrases are borrowed from *Lab Girl* by Hope Jahren (Fleet, 2016).

p.29: 'One of the many odd things about *Peanuts* is that you can't separate that distinctive line from physical and existential pain. Schulz lived with a condition called "essential tremor", which caused his hand to shake whenever he tried to hold it still.' Sam Thielman, 'Peanuts cartoonist Charles Schulz on the necessity of loserdom', *Guardian*, 28 Nov 2015.

p.34: 'I'm in my house listening to the owls calling' is from the poem 'Adult' by Linda Gregg, in *A Book of Luminous Things: An International Anthology of Poetry*, edited by Czesław Miłosz (Harcourt Brace & Co, 1996).

p.35: 'How to Catch and Manufacture Ghosts' is the name of a 1981 artwork by Alice Aycock.

p.37: The line 'What's it like to be always night?' is from the poem 'Notes on the Below' by Ada Limón. The lines 'has suffered an irreversible loss and talks about himself sometimes in the third person, sometimes in the second' and 'he has a friend, never named, who addresses him as Mr Bones' borrow from John Berryman's 1969 introduction to *The Dream Songs*.

p.42: The epigraph is from *Lorine Niedecker: Collected Works* (University of California Press, 2002). Flannery O'Connor wrote in her essay 'Living with a Peacock' (*Holiday* magazine, Sept 1961), 'I could sew in a fashion and I began to make clothes for chickens.'

p.46: Information and a few phrases in 'Exhibition (*Colour*)' came from *The Secret Lives of Colour* by Kassia St Clair (John Murray Press, 2016).

p.56: This is a found poem (almost all) composed of lines from *Girls Standing on Lawns* by Maira Kalman and Daniel Handler (Harry N. Abrams, 2014).

p.57: The phrases 'A pot explodes in the kiln, taking everything else with it' and 'Failure with clay is more complete and more spectacular than with other forms of art' came from *Urban Potters: Makers in the City* by Kate Treggiden (Ludion, 2017).

Mary Oliver is quoted as saying, 'I know the sag of the unfinished poem. And I know the release of the poem that is finished.'

p.62: The epigraphs are from Angela Epstein in the *Daily Mail* (14 Oct 2009), and the poem 'What is a Pineal Gland' by Anna Swir in *Talking to My Body* (Copper Canyon Press, 1996).

p.64: Helen Simpson is quoted as saying: 'I'd found you could be very happy and very miserable at the same time, and it's hard to describe that state.' Sarah Crown, 'Helen Simpson: "I stuffed it with sex and violence"', *Guardian*, 28 May 2010.

In 'Keeping Quiet', Pablo Neruda writes, 'Now we will count to twelve/ [. . .] / and not move our arms so much.'

p.66: The epigraph by Adrienne Rich is from 'Revolution in Permanence (1953, 1993)', in *Dark Fields of the Republic: Poems 1991–1995* (W.W. Norton and Company, 1995).

p.72: 'Whakairo' references information I learned while writing for *Ko Rongowhakaata: The Story of Light and Shadow*, Te Papa, 2017.

p.73: 'You Bury Me' is a translation of the Arabic 'ya'aburnee', from *Lost in Translation* by Ella Frances Sanders (Ten Speed Press, 2014).

p.76: Gwen Harwood is quoted in Simon West, 'Great Poem Hoax: *The Best 100 Poems of Gwen Harwood*', *Sydney Review of Books*, 6 March 2015.

p.79: The concept for 'Black Book Blueprint' came from Claire Messud, in *Light the Dark* (Penguin Books): 'I heard a frightening programme on the radio where a scientist was asked: "[. . .] In a millennium, say, down the line, what will survive of our world?" And his answer: Concrete. Maybe some glass. Well, what about paper? It will be carbonised, any book will be a black oblong object, the contents will be lost forever. All that literature and art and music, that's going to be gone. Of course, what we have from Pompeii is pots and pans – frescoes too – the hard goods. All the softer stuff is gone.'

p.81: 'Folding Tables' is made up of lines from exhibition labels (and one from a visitor interactive) at Te Papa.

p.83: The epigraph is from 'Poem Without an End', *The Selected Poetry of Yehuda Amichai* (University of California Press, 1996).

*

My thanks to the editors of *Sport*, *Cordite Poetry Review*, and *Best New Zealand Poems* 2015.

Thank you to my husband Eddie and our children. You are the light in these poems and *Museum* would not have become a book without your love. Thank you Mum. Thank you Fergus, Ashleigh, and Kirsten. Thank you James Brown. And thank you Te Papa Writing Team, for your aroha and friendship.